Charlie's Great Race

Story by Wendy Graham
Illustrations by Julia Crouth

Holly's dad kept homing pigeons in a loft in the back garden. Holly loved to help her father feed the pigeons, and she often put a bowl of water inside the loft for them to splash in. Her favorite pigeon was Charlie, because he would always let her hold him.

Dad belonged to a homing pigeon club, and he raced his pigeons against other pigeons. He thought that homing pigeons were special birds, because they could find their way home from long distances. Some of them could even fly faster than cars travel!

The homing pigeon club was about to hold its first race of the season, and all of Dad's birds were in training. Dad would take them out in his van, and then release them, so that they could fly back home. When they did, Holly would give them special food as a treat.

Each day, Dad released the pigeons a few miles further from home, so that they would get used to finding their way back.

On the day of the pigeon race, Dad left home early. He had to drive 60 miles to the starting point. The pigeons were in a traveling cage in the back of his van.

As Holly waved good-bye, she called, "Good luck, Charlie! I'll be waiting for you to come home." She hoped that Charlie would win the race.

Dad whistled as he drove along the winding road that led over the hills, and soon the city was far behind him. The pigeons were settled in their cage.

Suddenly, Dad slammed on the brakes. A dog had dashed out in front of the van! Dad swerved to miss it, but the van skidded across the road, and went over a grassy bank.

Small trees and branches snapped like twigs as the van bumped down the slope. Dad could not control the van, and it ran into a large tree.

Dad tried to move, but his legs were wedged tightly under the dashboard. He was trapped inside the van! His right ankle was very painful, and he thought that it might be broken. He had to get help as soon as possible.

No one had seen the accident, and it might be hours before he was discovered. He felt around for his cell phone, but it had been flung out of reach.

Dad managed to twist around to check that the pigeons hadn't been hurt. They were fluttering in their cage, but they seemed to be all right.

Then a great idea came to him. One of the pigeons could carry a message home to Mom and Holly!

Luckily, Dad had a pen and a notebook in his pocket. He wrote a short message:

He tore out the page and rolled it up. Then he reached back and just managed to open the cage door. He reached his hand over Charlie's back and lifted him out.

Dad tucked the message under the ring on Charlie's leg. Then he rolled down the side window and threw the pigeon into the air. "Fly home, Charlie," he called.

He was thankful that the sun was shining, because the clear sky would help Charlie to find his way home.

Charlie flapped his wings hard and soared upward. He recognized a part of the countryside that he had seen before, and knew which direction to take. He set off toward his loft, flying over the green forest, and following the curves of the hills. But he was still a long way from home.

Suddenly, Charlie sensed danger. The dark shadow of a hawk swept over him!

Charlie knew that it was going to attack, so he somersaulted in the air. Then he changed direction and dodged into the trees below. He had escaped—and not a moment too soon!

But as Charlie flew on, the sky clouded over, and large drops of rain began to fall. He couldn't see the ground clearly now, and for a short time he was confused. Then he recognized the silver line of a river. He knew where he was, and he headed for home.

Although the rain kept falling, Charlie reached the house at last. He swooped down into the loft.

Holly was in her bedroom when she heard the other pigeons making a fuss. She ran out to the loft to see what was disturbing them. To her surprise, she saw that Charlie was home already, much earlier than she had expected.

Then she saw that there was a piece of paper tucked into the ring on Charlie's leg. She caught him carefully. "Mom!" she called. "Charlie's home! And he's carrying a message!"

Mom came out to the backyard, and helped Holly to remove the note from Charlie's leg. "Oh no!" she cried, as she read it. "Dad's had an accident!"

Holly put Charlie in the loft, and then ran into the house. Mom called 911 and explained what had happened.

Holly went back to the loft with a special treat for Charlie.

Soon, Mom came out to the backyard again and called, "They've found Dad, Holly, and he's going to be all right."

"You saved Dad!" Holly told Charlie. "You're the best pigeon in the world!"